D1259533

SELECTED POEMS

SELECTED POEMS

By

GYULA ILLYÉS

Edited by Thomas Kabdebo
and Paul Tabori

1971
CHATTO & WINDUS
LONDON

Published by
Chatto & Windus Ltd
40 William IV Street
London WC2N 4DF

★

Clarke, Irwin & Co Ltd
Toronto

ISBN 0 7011 1540 8

WITHDRAWN

Original Poems © Gyula Illyés 1928, 1932, 1935, 1937, 1939, 1943, 1945, 1947, 1956, 1965, 1968

These translations © Chatto & Windus Ltd 1971

Foreword © Thomas Kabdebo 1971

All rights reserved. No part of this publica-
tion may be reproduced, stored in a retrieval
system, or transmitted in any form, or by any
means, electronic, mechanical, photocopying,
recording or otherwise, without the prior
permission of Chatto & Windus Ltd

Printed in Great Britain by
Redwood Press Limited
Trowbridge & London

PH
3241
.I55 A25

Contents

258967

YOUNGSTOWN STATE UNIVERSITY

FOREWORD

Gyula Illyés was born in 1902 at a small settlement called Rácegrespuszta, in Western Hungary. He came from a peasant stock of shepherds and agricultural labourers, though his father rose to the position of village mechanic. The economic conditions of his class were such, that it took the concerted efforts of his whole family to send him to secondary school, and his own exceptional gifts were needed to fight off the two-headed monster of poverty and social prejudice, barring his way to university.

When the waves of revolution reached Hungary in the wake of the First World War Illyés enlisted as a volunteer in the Red Army. The revolution failed and to escape persecution Illyés emigrated to Paris, where he lived for six years. He studied French Literature and Psychology at the Sorbonne and worked as a part-time binder and teacher to earn his living. But he never had any doubts of his real vocation: he wanted to be a poet. He made the acquaintance of Tzara, Cocteau and Barbusse, became a friend of Follain, Aragon and Eluard, and started to publish poems. He wrote in the *avant-garde* journals of Paris in French and in the publications of Magyar emigrants in Hungarian.

The decision to return to Hungary and become a Hungarian poet brought heavy obligations to Illyés, who interpreted the poet's task in the Petőfi tradition. "If you cannot do other than sing of your private sorrows and joys, you are not needed by the world, so put the sacred lyre aside," advised the great nineteenth-century revolutionary poet, whose best biography Illyés was to write in the thirties. Illyés believed that the people, and especially his own lot, "the blind and dumb peasantry", could talk only through its writers and poets. It was the primary duty of a poet to call attention to social injustice and political inequality within the society, but turn against external pressures when the nation was threatened by forces stronger than itself. Having fought through the period between the two world wars with his pen, on the side of the populists and other left-wing reformers, Illyés survived the German occupation of Hungary in hiding. After 1945 he entered politics and became a member of Parliament and a leading light in the Peasants' Party, but the increase of personality cult that gradually spread over Eastern Europe and finally burst into a reign of terror made him withdraw not only from his actual political posts but from other forms of public life as well. Yet he never resigned as a poet committed to improve on the position of his people, whatever form their oppression might take and however hard he had to look for ways of expressing his anxiety or finding the seeds of future optimism in the bitter fruits of events.

Meanwhile his strength and fame as a poet grew. His topics increased, his themes varied, his style happily assimilated the influences of surrealism and expressionism, and a basic, positive realism, palpable and entirely his own, emerged from the mould. From the early *Three old stagers* onwards the appearance of his volumes was welcomed by the public, prized by literary awards and hailed by fellow poets and critics. The most eminent of them, Mihály Babits, shared the editorship of the influential literary journal *Nyugat* (The West) with Illyés whose activities as an editor soon complemented his work as a poet and a writer of prose. When he gave up editing, at the end of the forties, he produced historical dramas, inspired by the same sentiments as some of his best poetry.

At the age of sixty-eight and still at the height of his creative powers Illyés can look back at sixteen separate books of poetry whose products have also appeared in six collected editions and in countless anthologies of Hungarian poetry at home and abroad. From the various collections published, László Gara's French-language edition is outstanding for its judicious selection and for the quality of its translations. This volume and the efforts of its collaborators earned the Grand Prix of Poetry for Illyés at Knokke in 1966.

Our selection of Illyés' poetry endeavours to introduce him to the English public through the most typical stages of his inner development as a lyric poet, increasingly conscious of his own standing. We hope that the undeniable pathos of his monumental poems, such as *Bartók* and *On seeing the Reformation Monument* and the wrath of his castigating pieces, such as *It did not help* and *A sentence on tyranny* does not stifle the voices of self-doubt, gentle irony and tenderness, ever present in Illyés' work. The frequency of horror, shock and subsequent contemplation proves that Illyés' poetic seismograph correctly registers the tremors of our century.

Two of the poet's best friends in England, László Cs. Szabó and Zoltán Szabó have helped us with their advice in choosing the poems from Illyés' still increasing *œuvre,* while C. Day Lewis has kindly vetted the translations to discard those he judged to be below the standard of the originals. Still, some problems of matching both form and content of the translations to those of the original verses remained only partially solved. The burden of keeping an intricate rhyme-syllabic-stress-scheme of the poems *It did not help,* of the *Reformation Monument* and of the excerpt *The three old stagers,* would have confronted the translators with difficulties beyond their powers to solve, if above all they had not wished to adhere to the meaning faithfully. So they sacrificed certain elements of form for the sake of content. The late Vernon Watkins, on the other hand, approached his tasks of translating *A sentence for tyranny* and *Fatherland in the heights* in the mode recommended by Pope and by Donne. Choosing the most suitable metre and never deviating from the general sense, he adopted expressions with more freedom than the other translators and made small modifications in the vocabulary, in the imagery, and in the structure of sentences.

11

The rest of the translations are the best approximations of Illyés' poems in English, which the present translators were capable of doing: all in the face of the heavy odds of a relatively unknown language and of a different poetic tradition.

THOMAS KABDEBO

What you have almost forgotten

What you have almost forgotten —
The speech of your quiet people — learn again!
More reviving than a glass of fresh water
Is their hearty welcome to the tired traveller,
A welcome that brims with friendly warmth.

See how here among the villagers waiting to be paid
You too nod agreement when they speak, as they
Tell of their destiny in their own rough words,
Give reasons for their poverty.
Eager life flutters birdlike
In the difficult movements of their lips.

In Kaposvár, in a young street which has no name yet,
On All Souls' Night a man asked me for a light —
    the wind
Blew as we huddled together, our coats over us,
As if embracing.
I looked into his face in the matchlight.
He smiled at me.
Our hearts recognised each other for a moment.

Another day I sat in a pub and a thin tailor
Asked to sit beside me, with such gusto as if
He were unpacking his good home-made lunch for me
    to share.
He unpacked his life before me
(The previous week a daughter had been born).

As the faces open to you, shine at you, your own
    face clears
And shines more warmly in the warmth of theirs.
Don't be ashamed
That you feel your grandmother's eyes

13

Are what you see with,
That your heart simmered like a happy samovar;
   it boiled
When you told good news to an old driver,
You felt the hot steam in your face
And stuttered of happiness.

On this dry, rough, rocky ground
The roots of your moods find the sweet earth
Through small crevices.
The openings are a happy smile,
The pupil of an eye that widened.

This soil will feed you. So that your song is like
The rustling of deep-rooted oak trees,
Like the heartbeats of the topmost leaves,
As they chatter, telling secrets
Of distant winds.

Tr. GAVIN EWART

The three old stagers (an excerpt)

Back since yesterday, here I am
home again in the old *puszta* —
so many memories and the pen in my hand
is at a loss for words.

And now, now that I've travelled down
all those roads that lay in wait for me,
my dead master, you'd see your pupil here
in need of your advice.

I really know what I should say
but, you see, the words
lie low and fearful in my soul
fluttering tentative wings.

Flashes of lightning and guns,
around me lies a dumb land,
a gasp breaks, they press hands to ears
who hear those sounds of pain.

Reach up out of your grave,
cover my hand with yours,
make me feel this line
half yours, half mine.

I have seen the world
and I, I too, reject it,
but still, my old uncle, let us still
raise up our hearts.

I too reject the world
but not with sad resignation
but defiantly and in anger —
my 'No!' is a cry to battle.

I didn't have paper with me
so I scrawled on the palm of my hand —
I seek to write of this dumb land
on the vellum of living hearts.

What I need is great, great courage,
and the aid of friends,
my ancestors' succinct words,
the fresh light of my childhood eyes.

Now at last it dawns on me
why I had to go to school,
why once long ago in tears
I had to leave my home.

Why my father had to work
and my mother to weep
and why it was that at parting time
you softly stroked my head.

Perhaps for this a hundred peasants,
now long dead, had to sing
and ponder as they ploughed: ●
that I should bring forth words.

Perhaps for this a bondsman once
choked back his rage and the pain
in the presence of his master,
so the bitterness should speak through me.

The whip cracked,
and the bondsman bit his lip
so that his cry should go up one day
full and clear to the skies.

Raise up your decayed hand
out of the count-ridden earth,
my old teacher, and you others,
point out to me the way.

I too say 'No!'
and cry against the world,
I cry and urge you all,
I look to a new dawn.

People of Hungary,
stepchildren of history,
rise up out of the *puszta*
to reconquer your homeland!

I stand here on the land
which was promised to you,
a groaning tree in the face of the storm,
bowing and waving.

Fly abroad, words!
Memories, cry aloud!
Blaze up, ye people, crackle and roar
— in *your* name I speak!

Stand behind me, Pál Czabuk,
you dictate the resounding words.
Be with me and if I'm punished
let me fall into your arms.

Tr. MICHAEL BEEVOR

Siblings

For three days, I would have only gazed
at the shaded valley of your eyes, your eyebrows,
    raised
above thick reeves of your lashes among which
tiny pools of lively waters itch
flashing their light, their agile schemes
the frolicking of little slippery breams.
For three days, as if on silence hooked,
into the one then into the other I'd have looked.

And another three days I would have spent
watching silently only the soft bend
of what is barely a hint under your dress,
and the little stars which slumber on your breasts
and prepare, arching the spokes of light,
to dazzle in the darkness of the night.
For three days, as if on silence hooked,
into the one then into the other I'd have looked.

And again, it would have been enough for me,
to graze my eyes on you, to watch you silently,
your twin knees, to a lovely stem growing,
and shyly challenging each other, drawing
like the double wings of a gate apart,
each other they might have encouraged: to part.
For three days, as if on silence hooked,
into the one then into the other I'd have looked.

In the mellow heat which gently poured
from your shining body I would soon have cured
myself, bathing in your light which shone,
on me, as on a sick man shines the sun,

watching stealthily, how in my chest
pain prickles and dissolves, and how the rest
of the body would itself dissolve into the sky
of an airier landscape, into a lullaby.

And I would have been a child, your child,
so that if I hug you, I'd hug you like a child,
that your tender voice could then be heard,
to get from you now the consoling word.
I hugged you so, brother his sister twin
the taste of ancient lust lessening the sin:
your most faithful lover, I was asleep fast,
by the time the first night, spent together, passed.

Tr. THOMAS KABDEBO

258967

YOUNGSTOWN STATE UNIVERSITY
LIBRARY

Bandit

His brows, like tousled bushes caught
in snow, the droop of his moustache,
while in the crevice of each ear
sprouted another snowy bush.
What hair he had upon his head –
retreating, hoary hair – was blown
like frosty sky swept by the wind
whirling above a wintry scene.
That I recall, and how his eye,
one good eye, like a winter sun
appearing, disappearing in
a frozen puddle, shyly shone.
His voice, too, like the winter wind,
or like that anguish hoarsely howled
by packs of wolves who far away,
and even now, are being killed.
He stood framed by the door. He wolfed
away at the huge mug of soup,
and with a somewhat shaky hand
wiped from his chin and chest each drop.
Then, humbly setting down the mug
before our gentle mother, he
wished us 'God bless', and stumbled off
towards the hill uncertainly.
He went, a fragment of a white
and winter's tale, hesitantly.
He went as he had come, upon
that close, oppressive summer's day.

Tr. J. G. NICHOLS

The apricot-tree

I

The apricot-tree
shoulder-high or less —
Look! an apricot
at branch-tip ripeness.

Stretching, straining,
holding out a prize,
the tree is a maiden
offering closed eyes.

You stand and wonder:
will she bend and sway
her slender waist or
step back, run away.

With quick breath shudders
from heat or passion,
fans herself, signals
in the high fashion.

Shakes the shimmering
pomp out of her dress,
then blushing she waits
for your compliments.

This garden a ballroom,
she gazes about,
anxiously, constantly,
wants to be sought out.

II

I spend each evening
all evening with her.
Come again tomorrow
she says in whisper.

She rustles softly
when I salute her.
It seems my poetry
can still transmute her.

Sweet apricot-tree,
in a dream I saw
the cool arbour, and you
on the crackling straw.

First you glanced around
anxiously, then left
the dark hedge, the well,
in your moon-white shift.

Your stepping increased
the silence gently,
brought me your body
soft and sweet-scented.

Since that dream I glance
towards you, flushing.
Please look at me too,
askance and blushing.

Tr. CHRISTINE BROOKE-ROSE

You cannot escape

We looked down into the ship's engine-room
where, among the pistons' steady beat
naked stokers scurried about
crimson as devils in the heat;
great gusts of boiling air escaped
the hatch as if from a door in hell —
What toil! I thought. . . but someone beside me
said: They're used to it, they know it well.

Sitting in a deckchair by the rail,
upon my lap a folded book,
blue mountains swam alongside, past me,
soothing my eyes, absorbing my tired look.
Hills and clouds of water — an unwritten
poem was all this, too — the slow
voyage — images woven in rhythms
to the muffled thumping below.

I swam over water, soared with the light,
happily knew I was beyond all now
high on the world's poetic stratum,
leaving below the unceasing row
of sweating and spitting and choking.
They're used to it, I told myself at last.
Or are they? And arrowing into me
came a cold sardonic shaft from the past.

Oh, are they? Did *you* ever get used to
(— you had a share in it —) that hoe?
Do you remember? Recall your father!
What did he get used to? His final blow?
In the midst of fate and poverty
what man can get used to anything?

Agonised, I paced up and down
on a ship's deck, feeling its writhing.

You are a fool, I told myself.
A traitor! just a traitor, nothing more,
amplified a voice in my heart,
while the moving deck groaned to its core:
Traitor! Liar! Miserable one!
Hireling, lying low! If once again
you found yourself among life's stokers
would you get used to the choking and pain?

I found myself against the rail
struggling, as if my father's fate
were cast beneath my feet, as if he stoked
again, day-labourer on the count's estate.
As if my father and all my ancestors
were toiling, panting, choking down below
and crying upwards from the grave —
the deck made knuckles rap against my sole.

Staring down at the water I saw
the blue landscape loping fast
away as if the motion weren't the ship's
but a panting history rushing past.
As if it flung at me its ragings,
sickening me, its pitiless No
— spelling it out — you cannot forget,
you cannot escape, wherever you go.

Tr. DOUGLAS LIVINGSTONE

Fatherland in the heights*

A time may come when to remember
Shall ask more courage than to plan,
To claim the past more than the future
In seeking a new fatherland.

What do I care? My land already
Holds, more than any height, all steady.
I walk, look around, live, nothing else:
I have found a weapon, magic spells.

I already share it, too, if I come
To tell you its nature, this secret home.
Murmur a line of Petöfi, friend:
In a magic circle at once you stand.

If this pure land's overrun by invaders,
A new Tartar horde or a horde of traders,
If our paths are twisted and made to squirm,
Just as when somebody treads on a worm,

Then speak to yourself, with eyes closed,
Just speak those words which at one time caused
Sands drifting, peoples, houses
To compose the pattern Hungary rouses.

Enraged rivers learnt gentleness,
Or defiant cliffs — do not forget this,
If we go back, proud-lipped, unsacred,
Into our fortresses, our secrets.

For mere chilling horror cannot chill us,
The merely murderous cannot kill us;

* This is the last translation made by the late Vernon Watkins,
which is included in this unrevised form. Had he lived he would
certainly have revised it.

Weave your bullet-proof vest of language right,
Declaim our Berzsenyi into the night.

Gather friend, all you learnt to see
When you walked in meadows which then were free,
All the spoil of the heart's and the mind's dominions,
In gay disputes, with girls for companions.

As Noah into the Ark brought kinds,
Bring every example of thought, the mind's,
The number of yearnings, orphaned, tell,
And your dreams' menagerie, as well.

Though for a thousand years to come,
Like an echo unchallenged, they lie quite dumb,
Your words shall answer the questioners' wonder
Then with the more surprising thunder.

Watch, then, and take the lesson to heart
Which is mute, though it reaches places apart:
Clasping my book in close embrace,
I look and laugh in my enemy's face.

For if I stand nowhere, I still can be
At home, at the heart of what I see,
Even if there my world is shown
Like a *fata morgana,* upside down.

So I remain a messenger here
With the precious graveyards in my care.

If the order to shoot me through the forehead
    is given,
Whatever there rests, escapes into heaven.

Tr. VERNON WATKINS

Rivers, fjords, small villages...

Waterloo, Wagram, Mohi — what were they
Before their mild and empty names were filled
With keenings, and a thousand deaths went sailing
Away to shell the overcast? Unskilled
We were in you, in fjord, hamlet, field
And equable river. And your fate incurred
Ought to have been, and ought to be today,
        To persevere unheard.

But thus the earth expands. New meadowlands,
New mountains in the mind of the child at school
Rise where gun barrels probe the map and point
To what they meant, being devastation's fool,
To erase from earth. The gun's a new ferrule
For the geography master, bright and burning
Milestone on the one old road that bends
        Towards one more turning.

One more, mankind? I who walked trusting by
Your side, now stand apart. Or do I plead
Against the tide, standing upon some whirled
Shipboard? If sin on sin is all the seed
Your learning sows, why then, my kind, indeed
Your servitude of spirit has to be
(An envious god's curse) endless. I shall cry
        As long as I can, my plea.

Be mute, Petsamo, bay and virgin hill
And you, secluded vales and homesteads; hounds
Couched to await a carcass like Sedan!
And you, small isles where Death the discoverer
  grounds

His keel, and an undreamed-of epoch founds!
Small places, new Americas, so long
Doomed to great fame, whose ruinous bounties
   swell,
           Be mute — nay, howl! Give tongue!

And see your destiny through. Come brighten,
   burn
And so many new stars! Ranked in armies, make
Not only history to a new design
But a new geometry on a sky in wreck.
And you, Petsámo, lurid bloody speck,
Rise, a new dispensation, on our sight:
That some time Man, in time to come, shall turn
       More hopefully, to the height. . .

                    Tr. DONALD DAVIE

Just not to have to die

Just not to have to die, you would consent
to live on any terms, and be content
to descend the ladder, rung by rung,
even to hoe turnips and spread dung.
You, a nobleman, and born as such,
would change with your own valet, lay your watch
and rings aside, settle for something worse —
to drive a waggon and to groom a horse.
And you, lord bishop, how you would roll up
your shroud-sleeves, just to keep the coffin top
from closing. While, great civil servant, you
would swing a shovel and be happy to!
We cannot tell where the dead disappear;
we'd prefer to lead oxen — and stay here!
Which of us would not serve (not just one year,
but a hundred) as a dog-catcher,
or, an old huckster on a muddy night,
drive a pony-cart without a light,
or, stepping further down, be glad to hand
bricks to a bricklayer's labourer, or to stand
outside on a street corner, in the cold,
washing guts, be a beggar woman, an old
woman even, and prepared to go
even lower; become an Eskimo,
a Negro, dwarf, idiot, and agree
to even lower forms — only to *be*!
Who would not leave this human shape and take
even a songbird's form, just for the sake
of living? be a raven, a quail, a wren,
a wolf, a tiger, a blind horse and then
perhaps a kind of vermin. . .a rosetree!
a rose, a blade of grass, which gradually

29

turn to their native meadows, having passed,
by gentle change, *to wet*, bare earth at last.

Tr. JOHN WILKINSON

Sacrifice

The lines I fashioned yesterday,
I have destroyed completely;
Lest they be found and I confess,
I will disown them neatly.
Today another thought arose,
An image longs to greet us;
But I am strangling this one too —
This living poem-foetus.
Still kicking, sense stirs inside you?
To life do you feel driven?
Are you a poem? Would you speak?
Then shout, corpse, up to heaven.

Tr. MARIE B. JAFFE

It did not help

Your house had been here — it burst to bits
this you can sense, yet don't understand
that your homeland had reached the same end;
the wonder is that it stood as long as it did:

Since it did not help our homeland
that your better digestion for supper
wished for the wine of these hills
and wished for the bread of these plains

And it did not help our homeland
that you smiled as you turned
and looked back there at the serf:
'How well he had put it — in Hungarian!'

And it did not help our homeland
that when the night came and you put down
    the book
and thinking of one of our heroes
you cried: 'he was the man. . . !'

And it did not help our homeland
that looking out of the window of the train
you would think well of the reapers:
'a better lot they should deserve.'

And it did not help our homeland
that even the thought was denied
that the three colours meant freedom,
brotherhood, equality.

And it did not help our homeland
that like heated spirits you let a few poems

of József and Ady and Tóth
through the nerves of your body.

And it did not help our homeland
to have a bouquet in the park
to stand by the statues and listen to speeches
and to make fireworks up the hills,

and after the supper in the vineyard
while mumbling into your glass
the tiger eye of your very red wine
looked back at you with the moon

and you wagged your finger towards the sky
— as this was done for a thousand years —
when the songs were sung
and images of famous paintings lingered about,

and enjoying the lust and the risk
— what you had said has come true —
you listened to forbidden radios
(and after: to gipsy music),

and the far sky above Hortobágy
and the shadow of the well with the double sweep
and your first king's crown adorning
the middle of all your coins,

and judged your father,
though called him 'dear',
and put a piece of Magyar pottery
on the wall of your room.

It did not help our homeland
it was not enough not to fall,

learn: that the wonder was nothing else
but the fact it hadn't fallen before!

By calling a mountain a king or a leader
— sticking their names on the top —
flattering, lies, just all the way through;
it was not enough for a home.

It did not help, it did not help
not to have faith and determination
that can mould a country together and weld
a generation into a nation.

And it did not help to have courage
though so many heroes had left their life,
one by one as a sacrifice,
that was not enough for refuge.

Since neither the strength nor the wisdom
might have been enough to have saved
the home whose dwellers had gone
because they could not find their place.

And it will not help for the time to come.
You have no home, and whatever you could build
would not be better than what had been, —
Scatter with the wind, cripples.

Tr. THOMAS KABDEBO

Horror

I saw: Budapest burning;
around a people's head
before its fall, a glowing
wreath of fire; war; war dead.

I saw — as if someone else —
amid wild briarbush
of exploding shell, a corpse,
a nightmare carcass, crushed.

There was moonlight that morning,
six o'clock, New Year's day;
the housewreck I was standing
on, at dawn, turned grey.

Like Moses' bushes, burning,
each shell, with rapid shriek,
burst, screaming something —
God or Fate tried to speak.

In the icy snow of the street
I saw a human head,
a bas-relief trampled flat
by some inhuman tread.

I saw a baby, still blind,
close to its dead mother:
not milk to suck but blood,
blood not wool for cover.

The baby raised its bloody face
and cried out to the dead.
His mother was —, this very place;
himself — the years ahead.

Tr. ANTHONY EDKINS

A sentence for tyranny

Where seek out tyranny?
There seek out tyranny,
Not just in barrels of guns,
Not just in prisons,

Not in the cell alone
Where third degree goes on,
Not in the night without
Challenged by sentry-shout,

Not where in deathbright smoke
Prosecutors' words provoke,
Not just in the emphasis
Of wall-tapped morse messages,

Not in confession told,
Not in the judge's cold
Death-sentence: 'Guilty!'
Not in the military

'Halt!' and the snapped-out 'Aim!'
'Fire!' and the drums of shame
Scattering the squad as it
Drags the corpse to the pit,

Not in the furtively
Guarded, and fearfully
Breathed words the message bore
Passed through half-open door,

Not in the 'Hush!' revealed
On mouth by finger sealed,
Nor confine tyranny yet
To rigid features set,

Peering through bars that still
Show, through that iron grille,
Cries that dumb throats retract,
Stopped in the cataract

Of inarticulate tears
Deepening the silent fears
In pupils griefs dilate
Darkened by looming fate,

Not only in 'Viva!' cries
Track down all tyrannies,
Surging on tiptoe, strong,
In the acclaiming song.

Where seek out tyranny?
There seek out tyranny,
Not just in mustered bands,
Tirelessly clapping hands,

Fanfares, and opera stalls;
Just as crude, just as false,
Monuments, art galleries,
Though cast in stone, speak lies;

Yes, each framed lie can crush.
Even in the painter's brush,
Or in the car with slight
Noise gliding through the night,

Where it draws up and waits
Throbbing in front of gates,
There, omnipresent, not
Less than your ancient God,

There seek out tyranny,
In school, in nursery,
In father's guiding rule
And in the mother's smile,

In, where a stranger puts
Questions that touch the roots,
Answering the stranger's gaze,
What the child always says;

Not just where barbed wire twines,
Not just between book-lines,
More than in barbed wire, in
Slogans that prick your skin:

There, more discreet, it is
In a wife's parting kiss,
Near you and at your back:
'When, dear, will you be back?'

In words that folk repeat,
'How d'you do's in the street,
Sudden, then, in the softer
Handshake a moment after

Making your lover's face
Found in the meeting-place
Freeze on the instant
Because it is present,

Not in the interrogation
Only, but love's confession,
In the words' honeyed wine
Like a fly in the vine,

For even in your dreams
You are preceded:
It had entered the bridal bed
And the desire it bred;

There's nothing you think fair
It has not already claimed;
Your bed it stole to share
Even when love was named;

It is in the plate, the glass,
In the nose and the mouth,
It is in the cold and the dark,
In the outer air and in your house;

As if through an open window
Came the reek of carrion
Or as if in the house there was
Somewhere a leak of gas.

Talk to yourself and hear
Tyranny your inquisitor;
You have no isolation,
Not even in imagination.

Through it the Milky Way becomes
A frontier terrain, scoured by beams,
A minefield, and the star
A spy-hole in a war.

The swarming canopy of the sky
Is a monstrous labour camp:
The Orator Tyranny
Speaks from bells on the ramp;

From the priest, to whom you confess,
From his sermon no less;
Church, Parliament, these
And the rack, are but stage properties:

Open and close your eyes;
Still its scrutiny lies
Upon you like a sickness,
Following you with memory's quickness.

Hark at the wheels of the train;
This is their refrain:
'You're a prisoner, prisoner, cast into jail
    by the binder.'
On the hill, by the sea, you inhale the same
    reminder.

In the lightning flash it is seen,
In every unforeseen
Little noise; its dart
Lights up your astonished heart.

Where you rest, there it is
In boredom's manacles,
In showers that forge nearby
Bars that reach up the sky,

In the snow, whose fall
Sheer as a cell wall
Hides you while tyranny looks
Through the eyes of your dog,

For it is in all you intend,
In your to-morrow it is at hand,
Before your thoughts it is aware,
In your every movement it is there;

40

As water cleaves the river-bed
You follow and form it; but instead
Of peering from that circle anew,
Out of the glass it looks at you.

In vain you try to escape its wrath:
Prisoner and jailer, you are both;
It works its own corrosive way
Into the taste of your tobacco,

Into the very clothes you wear —
It penetrates you to the marrow;
Detach your sense from it, you find
No other thought will come to your mind.

You look about, but what prompts your
    gazing?
You use your eyes, but what do they catch?
Already a forest fire is blazing
Fanned into flame by the stick of a match

Where carelessly you threw it down
As you walked, and forgot to tread it in,
And now it guards you in the town,
In field and home and the factories' din;

No longer you feel what it is to live;
Bread and meat, you do not know them;
You cannot have desire, nor love;
To stretch out your arms is now denied you.

Thus the slave forges with care
The fetters he himself must wear;
You nourish tyranny when you eat;
You beget your child for it.

Where seek tyranny? Think again:
Everyone is a link in the chain;
Of tyranny's stench you are not free:
You yourself are tyranny.

Like a mole on a sunny day
Walking in his blind, dark way,
We walk and fidget in our rooms,
Making a Sahara of our homes;

All this because, where tyranny is,
Everything is in vain,
Every creation, even this
Poem I sing turns vain:

Vain, because it is standing
From the very first at your grave,
Your own biography branding,
And even your ashes are its slave.

Tr. VERNON WATKINS
[Revised 1962]

At Plovdiv

Plovdiv, the Philippopolis of the ancients.
There too the Hotel Lamartine detained us
(It's that vast Greek-style place — no less would do
for the poet with his sixty horses and his retinue,
he talks of it at length, if I'm not wrong,
in his 'Voyage en Orient').
'Here is the room', said Peter, his tone heartfelt,
'where the great genius dwelt!'
'To tell the truth, it's overhead,' amended
the stockingless young matron, 'but the corn is
    spread
to dry up there, so nowadays it's our own
room that we show to the visitors, it must be said
this one's a good deal nicer.' And she showed us
the pieces put by for her daughter's bottom drawer
and all the family photos, an entire army
of spruced-up sons- and daughters-in-law, with a
    speech
on the mode of existence, past and present, of each.
She pointed out, among so many more
the poet too. 'We brought him down a floor,
mice swarm up there. And he's not out of place
here, poor thing — not a bad-looking face
his, either.' And she dusted off the likeness,
even as she invited us to guess
which of four holes it was, in a jug with four
handles to it, that the water poured from.
'Don't choose wrong,' she laughed, 'in case
you get a jet of water in your face.'
Only as we were parting from her was it
she showed us the right one, thanking us for our
    visit.

43

I gave a last look at the great
genius as he passed from sight,
telling myself: 'He manages here all right.'

Tr. DONALD DAVIE

Preamble

Between two hills, caught on exposed terrain,
The soldiers march on when the bullets rain.

They march on since there is no other road
And no other aim but to march on.

And that is how I came and brought my men:
The numerous intentions of my pen.

With my loyal ideals, with my stubborn care,
I am one and yet a hundred too, I swear.

A man for whom outer space is too small,
A Magyar — just a Magyar all in all.

Much-travelled, civilized and dull in turn,
A son of the *Puszta* who will never learn.

So many plans and roads our brains contrive,
Yet still one end — for after all, we die.

The troops which I have brought as all may see
Are the innumerable and single Me.

But when the hurricane of lead did fall
(And it may come down-pouring on you all

After youth with its hills and rills has passed
And has left you on flat terrain at last

With no cover or defence anywhere
Except what you yourselves from youth still
    wear),

Remember, *we* marched on! What gave us
    strength
Between beautiful youth and death at length?

Felled by doubt, reproach, error, derision,
The one fell and died but the whole went on.

However many wounded bled and died
The army has survived, and I survived.

For this death kills even the immortals,
And thoughts ran too, the cowardly ideals.

Yet in the troops which ebb but do not lag
I have also retained the ancient flag

Handed down by a better fate, or rather
a people — or just my shepherd grandfather,

So that in woe and wind it could resist,
And like a flame could chase away the mist,

And show through deeds — the true leader's
    command —
What honour, loyalty, ideals demand

From one who is alive. How much pain cries
And how much blood drips from these fervent
    lines,

From this heart which will be called to account
By completed time and the future's mouth.

Should I hide the pains which for you I paid?
No — so that you too should not be afraid.

Tr. R. BONNERJEA

Wild geese

The wild geese, starting off on geometry
      over again,
acutely angle their initial faint
      wavering line.

Even today that simple diagram —
      and autumn — still
have strength to startle me as though I were
      a boy in school.

The floating diagrams are drawn again
      and rubbed off by
a secret and self-pleasing hand upon
      the blackboard-sky.

Watching this cryptic formula take shape
      the thousandth time,
I ask 'Why go?' and know no better now
      than on our farm.

Autumn meant leaving, for a different world,
      mother and home.
'You'll grow away from us.' From everything
      loved and well-known.

I took the message, went, and I am now
      as I turned out,
troubled by what I'll never understand —
      what I am not.

The wild geese, working rapidly, evolve
      their old designs,
and honk by, as they did when I was young,
      in drifting lines.

Tr. J. G. NICHOLS

More daring I could have been, more free,
Prouder from the very first,
If you and I, my Hungary,
Could have had at least one sea-coast.
Then, in my youth, what dreams I could have
    nursed,
With all the longing of those days,
On cliffs, sloping sharply to the sea,
And below, all singing-living sighs
— Like a distant green-blue forest haze —
Infinity.

Then my soul would expand, take flight,
If thought at least could carry me
To islands still inviolate
Where it is summer continuously
And everything that is good is free,
If my narrow homeland, whose border
Is only dust and wire and stones,
Could break out in just one little corner,
Swamp all signs of artificial order,
All natural bounds!

Closely akin, blue water and blue skies,
One horizon blending into both;
Closely akin are daring and far space,
The fabled landscape and the time of youth.
Akin are the Pacific and that
Still more peaceful ocean,
Where, as islands, not Sumatra, but
Earth, Mars, Venus, Mercury, the Moon,
The wild Sun float!

Freedom, distance! Oh, if then
I had learned of you! Too late now,
This autumn night, a glass of wine
Before me on a stone table, below
A glass of water — Lake Balaton . . . So
I have come to this? I bow my head,
But the stubborn heart still whispers, 'Yet
You could stand up, follow where truth might lead
Out of this land, whose whole flood *you* would
   need
To wet your feet.'

How good it would have been! And how
The sky, shining with star-buoys, aches
Above me! Yet the mind will grow
Ever in suffering. Distance takes
The place of friend and brother, makes
Me fret, hemmed in by Hungarianness,
Homeland, age, (this triple wall),
I long for a new path, over newer seas,
Among the nations, and, having found all these,
New ports of call.

Tr. CLAIRE LASHLEY and JOHN WILKINSON

Bartók

'Harsh discord?' — Yes! They think it thus
          which brings us solace!
          Yes! Let the violin strings,
              let singing throats
learn curse-clatter of splintering glass
          crashing to the ground
          the screech of rasp
              wedged in the teeth
of buzzing saw; — let there be no peace, no gaiety
              in gilded, lofty far
          and delicate, closed-off concert halls,
              until in woe-darkened hearts!

'Harsh discord!' Yes! They think it thus
          which brings us solace!
              that the people live
              and have still a soul
their voice is heard! Variations on the curse
     of steel grating crashing against stone
              Though on the tuned and taut
              piano and vocal cords
          to stark existence their bleak truth,
              for this same 'harsh discord',
this woeful battle-cry disturbing hell's infernal din
              cries out
              Harmony!
For this very anguish cries out
— through how many falsely sweet songs — and shouts
          to fate: Let there be Harmony,
order, true order, or the world is lost,
          the world is lost, if the people
          speak not again — in majesty!

O stoic, stern musician, true Magyar
(like many of your peers — 'notorious')
was it ordained by law, that from the depth
of the people's soul, whither you descended
through the trumpet, the as yet mine-shaft throat
    of this pit, you should send up the cry
            into this frigid-rigid giant hall
        whose soft-lights myriad candles are?

Frivolous, soothing melodies played in my ear
                insult my grief:
let no light-tuned Zerkovic sing the dirge at this,
                our mother's funeral;
homelands are lost — who dares to mourn them
                with grind-organ arpeggios?
        Is there hope yet in our human race?
If this be our care and the reeling brain battles
                benumbed, speak, you
fierce, wild, severe, aggressive great musician,
        that — for all that! — we still have cause
                to hope, to live,

And that we have the right
        — for we are mortals and life-givers —
                to look all that in the eye
        which we may not avoid.
        For troubles grow when they are covered.
        It was possible, but no more,
to hide our eyes, to cover our ears
        while storms wreak their havoc,
and later revile: you did not help!

You do us honour by revealing what
        is revealed to you,
the good, the bad, virtue and sin —
        you raise our stature by
speaking to us as equals.
This — this consoles!
What different words are these!
        Human, not sham.
It gives us the right, and so the strength to face
        the harshest despair.

        Our thanks for it,
    for the strength to take victory
        even over hell.

Behold the end that carries us on.
Behold the guidon: by speaking out
        the horror is dissolved.
Behold the answer to life's riddle
by a great mind, an artist's spirit: it was worth suffering
        through hell.

Because we have suffered such things that still
        there are no verbs for them,
        Picasso's two-nosed women,
            six-legged stallions
        alone could have keened abroad
            galloping, neighed out
        what we have borne, we men,
what no one who has not lived it can grasp,
for which there are no words now, nor can be perhaps,

only music, music, music, like your music
twin lodestars in our sky of sound,
    music alone, music alone, music,
hot with ancient breath of mine-depths,
    dreaming 'the people's future song',
    nursing them to triumph,
setting them free so that the very walls
    of prisons are razed,
for bliss promised, here on earth
    praying with blasphemy,
sacrificing with sacrilege,
    wounding to cure,
    music now lifting
worthy listeners to a better world —

    work, a good healer, who lulls not to sleep;
    who, probing our soul
with your chord-fingers, touches
    where trouble lies,
and how strange, how wholesome is the salve you give:
    the plaintive call,
the lament which would spring from us,
    but cannot spring,
for we are born to dumb stillness of heart:
    your nerve strings sing for us.

Tr. CLAIRE LASHLEY

On seeing the Reformation
Monument, Geneva

I paced the length of it — one hundred and forty-three
paces from end to end. As a messenger
bearing the last salute of murdered millions
I passed along the line of stony faces;
Calvin, Knox, Farel, Beza! and those great bull-heads,
grim captains of embattled faith,
all those Williams, Colignys and Cromwells,
Bocskay with his battleaxe — how they looked at me!
It was all too much; I couldn't take them in!
I had to step back toward the garden, back
among the trees, back into the soul,
into that coolness where alone it is possible
to see a thing objectively and entirely.

And now, standing before me, at attention,
like so many soldiers on parade,
        they seemed almost
on the point of stepping forward
        out of the rock face
in which they stood,
out of Time, which had set
solidly at their backs.

Once they could move. Then they stiffened and became
stones in the sunlight. Their voices died away,
their words remain only in the form of deeds,
to provide a kind of explanation
somewhere in time . . . You who are dead,
you who stand at attention; speak!

        Or am *I* to speak first?

Must it always be with you as it always was —
'Here I stand; I can do no other.'
No compromise, whatever cause you serve,
for the lukewarm are spewed out of God's mouth,
while the right intention shall survive
like an object? How much truth is left
in those great fists which once, four centuries ago,
grasped a mighty oath and never once
released their grip, but stiffened into stone,
into eternity, their fingers still
grasping the Bible and the sword?
What did you think you saw
in the goal towards which you hastened,
pushing on with the rage of a lover
            as you drew near?
            Do you sometimes wonder?
But suppose the answer should not be to your liking?
Well, I shall give it anyway.
It's just as bitter for me as it is for you.

You stood there, burning with the truth of God,
while the opposing camp burned with the same fire;
then, for the thousand-and-first time,
       instead of reason,
weapons and a flame resolved
how the soul may reach eternal bliss
Bodies writhed by the million
on battlefield and scaffold,
the wheel, the stake and all the new
master devices for inflicting pain;
and opposing forests,
forests of the cross of Jesus,
sprang up all over Europe.

55

People burned,
in order that paintings, 'idols', should be burnt,
and the 'false Book' of the opposing party.
Cities and villages burned!
Half-savage mercenaries
devoured the flesh of men, fire met with fire,
crime with crime, until the final — Victory? —
Time, which awaited you, sagely, patiently,
                        with a touch of humour.
Now, today, in my country, as in yours,
the same two camps face each other still,
opposing fortresses gaze on opposing fortresses.
From ancient towers, austerely white or gold —
ornamented, opposing bells, like cannon,
peal out defiance to opposing bells,
every Sunday. And, inside, the priests
still thunder as they used to; but, after service
they wave across the street, signalling
at what time and at whose house this evening
they'll meet for a game of cards or a nice fish supper
with a few drinks.
                        Fair enough! I approve!
If I were a clergyman, I'd do the same!
'Live and let live' by all means.
                                And yet, you know —
those Thirty Years of Killing . . . wasn't it just
perhaps a little too high a price to pay?
D'Aubigné's fury, Coligny's death, the Night
of Saint Bartholomew still unavenged,
Germany, all Europe, torn apart,
and the Turk in our country
a hundred and fifty years . . .
So this was your 'victory'? God's way
of 'proving, like the sun', that the fight was not

for Him, but *because* of Him?
Was this the prize decreed to you by the future,
— since there could have been no victor whom He
had not *predestined* to his triumph?

                              You won.
The Devil won with you!
You were mugs, the lot of you! About turn!
You have no right to take even one step forward.
Crumble with your stone and with your Time —
Crumble! For the fight was lost
before it had begun.

Or perhaps I spoke harshly, like one who first
castigates himself with his own truth.
      So you failed.
The nett result, written upon the blackboard —
— the continent you wiped clean with your armies —
was the mere answer to a foolish riddle,
and that only possible in Hungarian,
where Protestants call themselves 'keresztyeny'
and Catholics call themselves 'kereszteny'
both meaning 'Christian'. And so the riddle runs:
'Why is a keresztyeny more than a kereszteny?'
Did you really require the blood
of so many millions dead, before
you could distill this particle of sense,
this little 'y', and when, forgetful of
your duty, you took up the sword and hacked
the Gordian knot of Christian brotherhood,
(keresztyeny hacking kereszteny),
and when you had cut so valiantly,
through the tangle of your own perplexity,
did you find it there, that little 'y'?
And were you satisfied with your 'result'?

But suppose none of this
had ever been? Then only inside myself
the two opposing bells would toll,
calling up for the thousandth time
the old bitter conflict, hardly less bitter
for finding expression only in the old
vile opposition of two words; 'word-wrestling':
then the shepherd of Tolna
would have kept the faith of his old Lord;
then the preacher of Sarret
must have endured the battle – in his own breast.

What made you take up arms?
Does not a virtuous man in his own right
furnish a proper answer to the wicked?
And if the battle had not been fought? If, wordless,
the Faith had perished in 'the Roman Filth'?
If the world and the ideal together,
led by the 'Church vendor with the tiara',
had gone where it was no longer possible
to speak against unrighteousness? Well, of course,
it would have been indeed heroic to say;
'Here I stand; I can do no other!' Of course
virtue would have made its sacrifice!
but hopelessly! And what would then have happened
to us? Would we have been spared the conflict,
the bloody sacrifice, the Inquisition?
            If – albeit 'in vain' –
Gustav Adolphus had not ridden,
if the Puritans of Toulouse had chosen
to submit rather than take up arms,
if the Vaudois, the Hussites and the free men
of Bocskay, who knew no word of Scripture
nor yet of prayer, had said; 'We will not fight' –

do you suppose we should then have had peace?
I almost see a patronising smile
crossing your stony faces at the thought of it!
And would we Magyars have been quite the same
if there had been no Calvin?
                              I don't think so.

Or put it another way: would you have had
electric light, had not Giordano Bruno
gone to the stake? Here was the beginning
of nuclear power — and when, some time tomorrow,
you take a rocket and fly out into space,
you will have these to thank for it, men
who were not daunted by the stake or the galleys
        or the certain prospect of defeat,
the 'in vain' that waits on every step.
They saw; they saw it well,
that there is no road leading to the past;
the past collapsed in smoke, hurling them forward
as the powder hurls the cannon ball.
they undertook the burden of their Fate;
then say with me: Glory be to them!

I stood before them, a speechless messenger,
hardly caring now what explanation
their deeds might have to offer, deeds, which, like
a child, can be reasonable for themselves
only when they're grown up.
Finally, as a self-consolation, I said:
     Whoever was responsible for the intention,
not even God could have made it otherwise.
                              Tr. JOHN WILKINSON

Bound for Szekszárd

The little train is puffing
up the hill;
expectant, a young woman's
sitting still.

Her eyes, at least, are lively
in their quest;
the kind of eyes that never
seem to rest.

Her forehead leans against the
window pane
and trembles to the rhythm
of the train.

She peers out, nodding as the
minutes pass,
a little sideways through the
sheet of glass.

How she is taking in the
countryside,
as though by proxy for her
unborn child.

Her eyelids flutter with a
smile demure,
like a young girl when tasting
sweet liqueur.

Her window-shaken face, with
gentleness,
appears constantly to be
nodding: yes.

Just see how she savours the
world again;
Across her eyes flit park and
lowland plain.

A country girl is she, her
glass beads tell,
and, with the beads, a little
cross as well.

Beside the cross her husband's
picture, see;
A pile of coloured brochures
on her knee.

Through her eyes run houses and
lines of trees,
and on her lips play fresh smiles
like the breeze.

Although her eyelashes are
open wide,
more along her mouth runs the
countryside.

All the cornfields and all the
sainfoin strips
appear to leave their taste
on her lips.

Bluish vineyards and yellow
stacks of corn
are caressing the sleeping
child unborn.

It hovers by virtue of
gentle bliss
within its mother and its
nation's midst.

This moment may decide its
destiny,
a finger may now touch it
secretly.

The whole world calls it but to
no avail,
as, from its shell, we used to
lure the snail.

Across my home county runs
now the train;
A number of thoughts, too, race
through my brain.

A little lady had once
borne me so,
my soul was being shaped here
long ago.

Gleaning all, the small woman
gazes, while
silently she creates and
grows her child.

Where she takes it, remains a
mystery;
it cheers me to be in her
company.

She's my landscape and on her
I survey
the marks of today and of
yesterday.

The little pregnant woman
fills my eyes
and I imagine: here my
future lies.

She carries a nation; like
contraband
she smuggles in a new Hung-
arian.

Perhaps in a young woman
years ago
Babits himself had seen my
mother so.

Did he think that in her was
being bred
someone who would treasure him
in his head?

My eyes feast on you, kindly
mother dear,
and I reflect; my native
land comes here.

Unaware, through whirlpool and
precipice
she is carrying Árpád's
heritage.

Perhaps the very soul she
hides inside
will speak my name one day when
I have died.

The source of ideal, of
thought and fear,
my eternity are you,
mother dear.

Forgive that mere watching you
makes me gay;
Now let me bid you 'god speed'
on your way.

Tr. JOHN P. SADLER

We listened. It calmed down, and — Do you hear?
  It's passed.
All gone the six months' roaring cannonade!
From far off a battle still belched once or twice,
then — though we almost wished to hear the sound —
there was no bang to start off the grenade,
there was no bang to mark its incidence,
there were no gunshots like croaks in a lake. . .
Just quiet, Q U I E T, Q U I E T! And this
                       sudden quiet
became new sensation, much more sensible
than the time when bridges splashed to sky
or the time when our house tumbled down;
this brought such a shell-shock to our heavy hearts,
that breathing stopped and look answered look:
can we survive?
            And we listened on but
there was only quiet, Q u i e t. And we lived.
It has broadened with amazing speed.
As the parachutist sees the earth rushing
towards him, we saw our future. And we lived.
Then with sudden gusto some significance
opened and blossomed out. We began to float.
Now it was a smooth ride, but still wondrous.
Oh that moment! This no man's moment of our age.
At the time of no man's lands, this *treuga dei,*
— land of no man's time — quickly fades away!
Up to then we drifted from those odd deserters
and those persecuted Jews we had about,
but at this moment they became like us.
What equality oh, what renewal
was promised by this soundless moment,

65

this eardrum-strain of ancient silence
worth a Beethoven-like symphony!

Tr. M. SÁRKÖZI

Charon's boat

Our trip in Charon's boat does not begin that day
When eyes are closed in everlasting sleep;
Aware and open-eyed, we transients sail away
Across the fateful deep.

Long years before our envious fate embarked upon
The journey ultimate — of no return —
The ship, responding to our every whim, sailed on,
Wonder at every turn.

Past beautiful canals, mysterious lagoons, —
Familiar route, as if we had rehearsed;
The sky, the gentle landscape, fit for honeymoons —
All scenes are in reverse!

And all is fresh and lovely; more intriguing
The pictures, as before our eyes they spin;
Just as a tune is sweeter upon leaving
The singing violin.

We sit among the trees, with friends we gaily laugh —
When suddenly the boat begins to rock;
The time has come for us — an end to talk and chaff —
We recognize the knock.

He is a sage, who on this trip accepts his fate;
Who smiles; or weeps with tears of gratitude,
For all the treasures he has shared of late,
During his Interlude.

Tr. MARIE B. JAFFE

Rain at the end of spring and black cloud,
and a fire in the stove still needed
in a house pushed by the mountain wind
where I survived to the winter's end,
where the stove is cold; my overcoat
is hardly keeping the weather out.
Bones and coat against the window-sill,
I suffer the edge to penetrate
as if to distract my sickened heart
which questions why I should live at all.

The fierce rumblings of Lake Balaton
shake the dusk; its fanged rush leaps along
to burn mad-houses, to raze the sties,
force pent-up screaming and the harsh cries
of a goaded monkey-pack. At times
words I can understand in the din:
a human voice but filling the sky
shouts, 'Hurry!' then choking, 'After him!'
then, 'Look out!' then louder still, 'Why try!'
then laughing, 'You helped it to happen!'

The storm's tumbling cacophonies cross
the sequences I seek, the statements
I listen for: these thrown voices are
mirrors flashing, mirrors that I hear,
reflecting with sudden prophecy.
What do they show us? What kind of face
wavering from the despondency
and numbing cold of the soul's blind base?
Inside and outside aching alike
over the ruins, Carthage, a life

breaking beyond my reparation;
and rattling round its celebration
my poem, tensed, a frenzied shaman
but praying for calmness to come down.

Tr. ALAN DIXON

Mother Sun

After the artificial warmth of wood
and coal, a stepmother's measured
warmth which, like our daily bread,
we have to earn sweating, how good

this udder-warmth is, this milk-warmth
that the central heating of the sun,
burning again, causes to run
into bent vessels of blood and lymph.

All my pores drink it greedily.
This is what is really free,
pouring into us, thick and fast as ever!

It permeates me so, so much grace
makes me believe we must, in some place,
have an eternal mother.

Tr. ANTHONY EDKINS

Eve

Like the rib which, to make Eve,
    was torn from Adam's side,
so I carry a secret,
    awesome virgin bride:

my death! — the most faithful, most
    carnal lover I know;
the best trouble-soother and
    eraser of sorrow.

It's not solitude that waits!
    My partner stirs in me.
The nuptials the most ancient
    and most complete shall be.

Though but part of me, she stirs
    and vaguely gives a sign;
she will fulfil the purpose
    for which she's been assigned.

A woman's body will leap from mine,
    her arms clasping me tight.
It will be an awesome miracle
    but a natural sight.

Tr. JOHN P. SADLER

Caravan log-book, found

Only the compass kept on hoping,
   it stuttered: showing
signs with its paralytic tongue: somewhere
   something answers there.

   And on we went
again through a dayful of desert.

A stone wall we found with its
   hieroglyphs.

Line upon line, stubborn: mad
wrinkles upon a forehead.

   Ancient decay,
Time struggles here

It has nothing left to say.

   So only the winds jeer.

Sand between the sweating fingers. Sand on the eyelashes.
   Sand when tooth with tooth touches.

We killed our camel who knew the way.
We had our last dinner today.

Tr. THOMAS KABDEBO

My sensors

My fingers knew how to smile
on your breasts,
to trust in your palm,
to accept your back.

They knew how to remake me
— a prisoner of pride and suspicion —
that out of the crucible
we could be reborn as twins.

   There were words,
   looks and sighs
   that showed you my past and my future. . .

Now the new heart
they transplanted within me is clean
— my fingers, fond allies

your face made noble.

Tr. DOUGLAS LIVINGSTONE

The street from the Ujlaki church in Old Buda is almost as broad as a square. The one-storey dwelling houses are lower there than usual. Once the road was on the level of the windows like some permanently maintained flood. At dusk one Friday a lanky well-dressed woman came out from such a house, an inn that was still privately owned. Her eyes were huge and round and she was blind drunk. She swayed gracefully. The blocks of the wide cobbled street teased her by saying that they came from a mountain stream where they had once been stepping stones and that was why one had to step on every other one. This was self-evident since the stones were wet. It was raining; steadily and heavily and, although it was November, like a tropical storm. The light of the street lamps cut the pouring rain into streaks. The separate strands of the woman's dishevelled hair were like so many drain pipes.

She was soaked to the skin, but she did not feel a thing. Otherwise she would not have tried to push aside the rain as if she had been in a marshy area parting the reeds, or as if she had been coming out from a bead curtain in a hair-dresser's shop. Only after one large curtain came another and another; ten, twenty, a hundred, miraculously thousands upon thousands.

All the same it was obvious that this was make-believe. What was really happening was that the woman was walking between hanging tendrils in a primeval Brazilian forest and, on the trees above her, were many multi-coloured parakeets, grimacing monkeys, swarming snakes, but these ones were so savage that they do not exist in South America and only went there on this special occasion. Who therefore would not have thought of helping her at such a time? According to Chateaubriand, it is the most exciting thing in the world to start an adventure with a native woman in this way. Yes — but we do not take account of the distances in the primeval forest. According to my experienced seaman's eye we were at least a mile apart.

Tr. NEVILLE MASTERMAN

Tilting sail

The tall canvas tilts the mast
      and the sail spreads
to reap the foam when the boat
      plunges ahead.

Look — when is it mast and sail
      fly forward most
victoriously? When bent
      at their lowest.

Tr. ANTHONY EDKINS

The edges of the hatchets were heated on a gas flame, in a roadside mounting shop and hammered cleaver-wide.

The tree-stumps brought on lorries and carried across these new provinces, grimly, speedily, undeterred: almost following a ritual.

For they arrived at any time, at high noon or deep midnight, to any random place among these unclean settlements,

where women did not prepare food, did not make up beds as theirs did, where men did not greet them as their custom, where the children and the whole godforsaken company did not pronounce speech as they did, where the circle drew aside from them,

they took twelve men, preferably young ones, of this unendurable, insolent people to the market-place,

and there — because of blah-blah and also on account of rhubarb-rhubarb, they were whipped and then beheaded,

necessarily because of ho-hum and naturally bang-bang,

and expertly for they were rather different as to their occupations,

agronomist and butcher, bookbinder and engineer, waiter and doctor, several seminarists, cadets from military academies, in general lots and lots of students,

familiars of Carnot, Beethoven and even Einstein, displaying their finest talents,

for after all plim-plam-plim and oh-lala,

while records were broadcast through loud-

speakers and now and then an irritable command
and they, the zealous ones, wiped their foreheads
and now and then turned aside to urinate for
excitement affects the kidneys,

    then carefully washing the tree-stumps and hauling
down the great tricolor which still waved at such
times over their heads,

    they marched on towards the wide future, too

    passing among the heads, carefully placed in a
circle,

    then from the settlement where now, too,

    and afterwards and forever,

    reason, compassion, hope have gone,

    krrrr, krrrr, rrrr. . . .or rather arr,arr, that sound
that now alone,

    without music, without words, monotone,

    the needle traces on the stopped record like a hone.

Tr. PAUL TABORI

Ode to a lawgiver

A Jubilee greeting to Tersánszky

The law could be right and valid for everyone,
If we human beings could be cast
Like adobes by the billion
From the same mould, the first one like the last.

But what must be must;
Every heart has its separate way,

And for some time now,
We have been more than clay and clay.

I will be plain, as only a writer can,
In whom the scholar and the judge are one,

And sing of something new.

Let there be law, a living law
In which all men cohere and none conflict,

Whose total force may draw
The partial truth of one, yet not restrict
The movement of the one within the whole
— As an adobe in a mould — but let
Each, like an atom, freely circulate,
In its own sphere within the general soul.

Existence should create order, not sorrow!

All power, then, to the shade, whose form
May hold the blueprint of tomorrow,
To the exception
From which tomorrow's rule may follow

And to the poet, the man most fit
To experiment; let him be free for this,
Does it require less talent than to seek out
A cure for cancer? Less
Creative zeal
Than to harness the atom's power to a driving wheel
Or cross the brink of outer space,
To discern, ripening in the mind,

The form of future days,

To lay bare, as with ultra-violet rays
Tomorrow's rule for all mankind
Outlined in embryo?
What the nerves apprehend but cannot know?

This form the distance of a milliard years!

All power to the surgeon's knife
Which turns back the false surface and lays bare the
    life,
Separating each minute the bare tissue
From the live,
Putting things right, alert for every issue,
Every latent force, whence may derive
This man's murder
That man's thievishness,
How beauty is deformed,
How the deformed grows beautiful,
Whether he who is termed
'Leader' is a hero or a clod —

Since there's no royal road
To acceptance in our time;
So many curious facts emerging —

Words from the dumb,
The hunter being pursued,
The lewd woman a virgin
And the virgin lewd.

Not all creative beings are like that,
But I believe that those who must proceed
And fight after this fashion, are the ones
Whose formations we most need
To watch for, the reconnaissance
In whom tomorrow's battle lines appear.
Before them, Anna Karénina, Bánk, Hamlet
Dance like flames in the upper air,
Fantastically clear.

The ancient world takes on a rare
Lustre from their tones.

All hail! then, to those who bear
Law and light within their bones,

Men who will face the stake, the mocker's sneer,
Even failure — and still press on,
Whether they quite know why or not.

Let us salute Jenö Tersánszky, then,
For the journey he made and the truth he brought.

Vivat!

Sing on, master of many voices! Build
Your collapsible dinghies, plan
Your ancient reed pipes, new brakes for bicycles, gild
Your divinely useless gadgets,
Your total man
In all his crazy details!

Never take your arms and mind and mouth from the
    task.
Long may you work, be happy! But take care,
That — like this century — you never ask
Who you are!

Tr. JOHN WILKINSON

To the trees

Now, at last, you must leave us, dear companions,
trees, the sharers of our summer joys,
the slender poplar and the portly walnut
who drank with us the gold of sunlit days,
hornbeams, beeches, nourished by the sky
from the same kitchen as ourselves, who were
our foster-brothers, not in milk but light,
brothers in heat and soil, cloud, matter, air,
loyal homeland trees, the alarms of parting
are at hand; showers of sharp steel
needles have come whirling down since morning,
flung out, from the snowstorm's giant wheel!
Snowstorm! Twenty degrees of frost! The meadow
heaves in chalkwhite waves, all creatures run
who can; the sudden flood drains from the landscape
as sudden-swiftly as it had begun:
men run as if they were drowning; the house is now
an island (a southern one if heated!) the dog
sits and howls on the snow-foamy threshold
and flocks of birds take refuge in the stack.
Only you, the trees, stand out unshaken
if the chalkwhite sea, this moonscape which
stabs us to the lungs, bites like a dagger
into our inmost flesh, but cannot reach
you, happy amphibians, who endure
this other element, able to breathe
what (like the atmosphere of outer space
or the pre-human earth) would mean our death.
You button up your cloaks of bark around you,
you send your tepid bloodstream spreading through
from the limbs, the crown and down the trunk

into the root, and what is it to you
how far this planet strays from the sun's circle
into what cold? you — who know what awaits
all life on this grim soil, ruled by necessity —
merely suspend existence when it hurts!
Heroic, primeval strikers! For where's the sense
in living otherwise than without pain?
Tenacious ones! You have always won through the
    frost,
to see the snow melt round your feet again.
. . . It is sad to leave you, full grown trees! bushes!
hedges! Though ice tinkles and hoar-frost glares
from your branches, I feel you growl defiance;
you live, like denizens of other stars!
wise brothers who turned to other paths, or, like
so many Abels, kept to the old roads,
— true to the same old faith, 'one flock, one
    shepherd' —
whom Cain's accursed breed murders, denudes
and may exterminate at last, in order
day by day to place a log upon
the stolen fire of its own shivering race . . .
mutilated corpses every one!

Tr. JOHN WILKINSON

Old men pursued

Away Tolstoy began to run,
not from death.

Did he run down

  from the summits,
the same direction as Móricz
whose old stick took a new lease
of life? He taught prevention of frost. He'd say
make your own bricks, show his peasants the way.

'If there is some small thing that I can save.'

  Old men, like saints
touched by an angel on the shoulder,
sent on your way, but with what order?
  How? Never against

  your own wishes.
  Who could compel you?
  Whose message tell you
to forget yourselves?
No word from a god, or doctrine
  of fear made you run
  from your fellow-man
  to know his house and bad fortune.

We are reminded of student days
and the smell of winter ending; youngsters,
moon-governed, our noses bled with regularity:
now we are drawn to the valleys, disturbed
  by perching on the heights,
seeing the breathless way ascended.

The fields and houses below, where death is known
    as an animal is known.

I will not hold my hat and stick
too easily when I must take
the down direction when a whistle blows;
led by my dogs, my oddities,
my happy pack
            of barking fools! . . .

Tr. ALAN DIXON